EASY JAZZ DUETS FOR 2

TROMBONES

To access audio visit:
www.halleonard.com/mylibrary

Enter Code
2868-3524-3160-2327

ISBN 978-1-59615-461-2

Music Minus One

EXCLUSIVELY DISTRIBUTED BY

Hal•Leonard®

7777 W. BLUEMOUND RD. P.O. BOX 13819 MILWAUKEE, WI 53213

Visit Hal Leonard Online at
www.halleonard.com

The Green Danube

NORMAN FARNSWORTH & WILLIAM MINOR JR.

Easy

♩ = 152 2 bar drum intro.

Tone Colors

NORMAN FARNSWORTH & WILLIAM MINOR JR.

Easy

♩ = 88   2 bar bass intro.

3

Reaching Up

NORMAN FARNSWORTH & WILLIAM MINOR JR.

Easy

Uptown-Downtown

NORMAN FARNSWORTH & WILLIAM MINOR JR.

Easy

♩ = 126 2 bar drum intro.

5

Main St.

NORMAN FARNSWORTH & WILLIAM MINOR JR.

Ski Slope

NORMAN FARNSWORTH & WILLIAM MINOR JR.

Easy to Medium

♩ = 108   2 bar drum intro.

Doin' Your Chores

NORMAN FARNSWORTH & WILLIAM MINOR JR.

Easy to Medium

♩ = 138   2 bar bass & drum intro.

Stop and Go

NORMAN FARNSWORTH & WILLIAM MINOR JR.

Easy to Medium

Glider

NORMAN FARNSWORTH & WILLIAM MINOR JR.

Easy to Medium

Jumper

NORMAN FARNSWORTH & WILLIAM MINOR JR.

Easy to Medium

Da Dit

NORMAN FARNSWORTH & WILLIAM MINOR JR.

Easy to Medium

♩ = 126   2 bar drum intro. (pick-up)

8va basso optional

Hot Fudge

Tijuana

NORMAN FARNSWORTH & WM. MINOR JR.

Medium

14

La De Da De

NORMAN FARNSWORTH & WM. MINOR JR.

Medium

Switcharoo

NORMAN FARNSWORTH & WM. MINOR JR.

Medium to Difficult

Swing Easy

NORMAN FARNSWORTH & WM. MINOR JR.

Medium to Difficult

♩ = 116 2 bar bass & drum intro.

Hop Scotch

NORMAN FARNSWORTH & WM. MINOR JR.

Medium to Difficult

Swingin' In The Rain

NORMAN FARNSWORTH & WM. MINOR JR.

♩ = 108 2 bar bass & drum intro. (pick-up).

4/4 Waltz

NORMAN FARNSWORTH & WM. MINOR JR.

Medium to Difficult

♩ = 168 2 bar drum intro.

One Note Break

NORMAN FARNSWORTH & WM. MINOR JR.

Medium to Difficult

♩ = 176 2 bar drum intro.

Lazy

NORMAN FARNSWORTH & WM. MINOR JR.

Medium to Difficult

♩ = 112 2 bar bass intro. (pick-up)

Bits and Pieces

NORMAN FARNSWORTH & WM. MINOR JR.

Medium to Difficult

♩ = 152 2 bar drum intro. (pick-up)

MORE GREAT BRASS PUBLICATIONS FROM

Music Minus One

CLASSICAL PUBLICATIONS

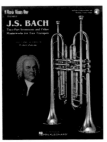

J.S. Bach –
Two-Part Inventions
& Other Masterworks for
Two Trumpets
Trumpet Edition
Performed by Robert Zottola
Book/Online Audio
00124386 ....$19.99

W.A. Mozart –
Horn Concertos
No. 2 in E-Flat Major, KV 417
No. 3 in E-Flat Major, KV 447
French Horn Edition
Performed by Willard Zirk
Accompaniment: Stuttgart
Festival Orchestra
Book/Online Audio
00400388 ....$19.99

Igor Stravinsky –
L'Histoire du Soldat
Performed by Gerald Kocher,
trumpet; Sean Mahoney,
trombone
Accompaniment: Parnassus
00400442 **Trumpet**.......$19.99
00400452 **Trombone**....$19.99

Advanced
Trombone Solos
Accompaniment: Harriet
Wingreen, piano
Book/Online Audio
00400694 **Volume 1**.....$14.99
Book/CD Packs
00400149 **Volume 2** $14.99
00400738 **Volume 3** $14.99
00400739 **Volume 4** $14.99
Downloadable Edition
01007390 **Volume 5**.........................$14.99

Intermediate
French Horn Solos
Performed by the Jersey State
Jazz Ensemble
Downloadable Editions
01007043 **Volume 1**......$14.99
01007325 **Volume 2**......$14.99
01007327 **Volume 3**......$14.99
Book/CD Pack
00400395 **Volume 4**......$14.99

JAZZ/STANDARDS

20 Dixieland
Classics
Trumpet Edition
Performed by John Hoffman
Accompaniment: The Dixieland
All-Stars
Book/Online Audio
00400617 ....$14.99

Play the Music of
Burt Bacharach
Performed by the Jack Six
All-Star Orchestra
Book/Online Audio
00400647 **Trumpet**.......$14.99
Book/CD Pack
00400651 **Trombone**....$14.99

Classic Ballads
for Trombone
Trombone Edition
Performed by Ira Nepus
Book/CD Pack
00131620 ....$14.99

From Dixie to Swing
No. 1 in D Major, No. 2
in A Minor, No. 3 in G Minor
Performed by Dick Wellstood
All-Stars
Book/Online Audio
00400619 **Trumpet**..........$14.99
Book/CD Pack
00400622 **Trombone**.......$14.99

The Isle of Orleans
Performed by
Tim Laughlin's
New Orleans All-Stars
Book/2-CD Packs
00400446 **Trumpet**.......$14.99
00400461 **Trombone**....$14.99
00400503 **Tuba** $14.99

New Orleans Classics
The Chicago & New
York Jazz Scene
Performed by Tim Laughlin's
New Orleans All-Stars
Book/2-CD Packs
00400025 **Trumpet**.......$19.99
00400026 **Trombone**....$19.99

Music for Brass
Ensemble
Performed by Tim Laughlin's
New Orleans All-Stars
Book/CD Packs
00400432 **Trumpet**.......$14.99
00400451 **Trombone**....$14.99
00400519 **Tuba** $14.99
Downloadable Edition
01007040 **French Horn**.$14.99

Play Ballads
with a Band
Performed by the Bob Wilber
All-Star Band
Book/CD Packs
00400645 **Trumpet**.......$14.99
00400649 **Trombone**....$14.99

Signature Series
Trumpet Editions
Performed by Bob Zottola
Book/CD Packs
00138903 **Volume 1**.....$14.99
00142697 **Volume 2**.....$14.99
00147464 **Volume 3**.....$14.99

Swing with a Band
Performed by Steve
Patrick, trumpet; Roy
Agee, trombone
Book/CD Packs
00400646 **Trumpet**.......$14.99
00400650 **Trombone**....$14.99